Design
for
Living

Eichler Homes

The former residence of Joseph L. Eichler, founder of Eichler Homes.
Designed by Anshen & Allen and built in 1950 and 1951.

Design for Living Eichler Homes

Jerry Ditto Lanning Stern
photography by **Marvin Wax**

Introduction by
Sally B. Woodbridge

CHRONICLE BOOKS

SAN FRANCISCO

Printed in Hong Kong.

Book and cover design: Lanning Stern

Library of Congress Cataloging-in-Publication Data:
Ditto, Jerry
Eichler homes/by Jerry Ditto, Marvin Wax, and Lanning Stern
         p.   cm.
Includes index
ISBN 0-8118-0846-7
1. Eichler, Joseph L., b. 1900. 2. Industralist—California—
Biography. 3. Construction industry—California—History
—20th century. 4. Prefabricated houses—United States—
History. I. Wax, Marvin. II. Stern, Lanning. III. Title.
HD9715.U52E373 1995
338.7'6908'092—dc20
(B)   94–41851
                                            CIP

Distributed in Canada by Raincoast Books
8680 Cambie Street
Vancouver, B.C. V6P 6M9

10 9 8 7 6 5 4 3 2 1

Chronicle Books
275 Fifth Street
San Francisco, CA 94103

Other photos of the former Eichler residence provide a glimpse of the architecture and design for living Mr. Eichler wished to bring to the California home buyer. In addition to Anshen & Allen, two other architectural firms—Jones & Emmons and Claude Oakland & Associates—provided classic post-and-beam, open architectural design for Mr. Eichler and Eichler Homes until the year of his death, 1974.

Contents

What he
wrought–
the
Eichler Home
–was a product
of his
aesthetic,
his
eye
for design
and color,
his
feelings
for things
contemporary,
and
his principled
and
sometimes costly
appreciation of
design
elements
over
pragmatism.

Foreword
Jerry Ditto

One of many quintessen-
tial Eichler homes that are
found in over thirty-three
cities in Northern and
Southern California.
The rather simple, stark,
rectilinear facade of this
design stands in interesting contrast to the open,
floor-to-ceiling glass walls
of the interior and rear.

This book is about the art and architecture of Joseph Eichler, home builder. Mr. Eichler built something that had never been built before and has never been built since—classic, award-winning, architecturally designed homes for the individual or family of average means. He did so in well-planned, relatively large tract developments as well as in smaller enclave areas of nine or ten homesites. And he did so with a style and verve that is still remembered to this day—almost forty-five years after the Eichler phenomenon began.

If the phenomenon began serendipitously, it ultimately prevailed because of Mr. Eichler's principled and often irascible approach and because of his team of extraordinarily talented architects. The architectural firms of Anshen & Allen and Jones & Emmons, both of whom achieved national and international reputations, and later the firm of Claude Oakland & Associates, provided Mr. Eichler with the careful architectural design of the classic post-and-beam idiom that remains fresh and contemporary to this day.

While this book is principally devoted to Mr. Eichler's buildings and the timeless quality of those creations, a glimpse of his personality is apropos. Although I never had the good fortune to meet Mr. Eichler, I have become acquainted with his son, Ned, and Ned's son, Steven. In addition, I've met and visited with a number of past associates of Mr. Eichler, former employees of Eichler Homes, and Eichler homeowners who knew him. What emerges from these recollections is an often irascible, larger-than-life character. Genuine respect and admiration for the man always appears as stories are told and retold about his early and bold principled position on the sale of his homes to anyone, no matter their color or creed.

If he was perhaps a less than gracious man, the passage of time seems to have softened the recollections of those who had occasional run-ins or differences of opinion with him. For example, a story was told about a dispute between a homeowners association and Mr. Eichler over the exact financial responsibility and ownership of the pool/community center. As the storyteller continued with his recollection, the event seemed to take on less sizable proportions, and he finished by acknowledging that "...of course, Mr. Eichler ultimately did the right thing for the homeowners."

This larger-than-life image has been chronicled, perhaps romanticized, in many newspaper and magazine articles in the San Francisco Bay Area

These two-shed roof designs by Jones & Emmons allowed for floor plan variations, depending on site placement. For example, the garage in the home at top is located at the extreme right; in the home below, it is at the extreme left. Virtually all Eichler homes were built using reverse or mirror-image plans in order to achieve even greater diversity in exterior appearance.

The high-pitched gable roof becomes a focal point of the street-level view of this Claude Oakland design. More often than not, Eichler homes were situated on level lot sites.

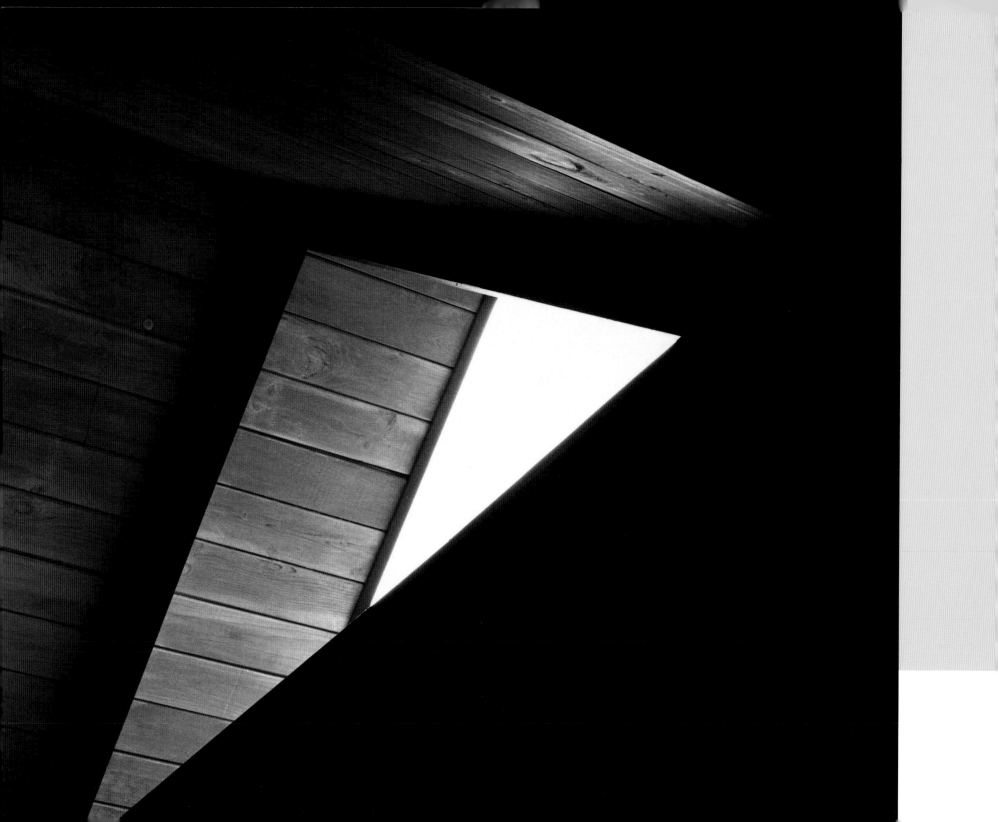

and elsewhere over the years. Stories about Joe Eichler and his homes began in the early 1950s, when the houses first became known as "Eichlers," and continue to this day—strong evidence that "what Joe Eichler wrought" was in fact something quite beyond notable tract home development.

What he wrought—the Eichler Home—was a product of his aesthetic, his eye for design and color, his feelings for things contemporary, and his principled and sometimes costly appreciation of design elements over pragmatism. Remember, as you view the images in this book, that the glass walls and open floor plan of the Eichler, while not necessarily so unusual or striking today, were indeed unusual and very unlike the normal modest tract home forty-five years ago. Tract developers would normally base their business on proven and safer designs of easier construction, such as "Cape Cod" designs or the "Ranch" home with large picture windows. But not Joseph Eichler.

The "Eichler Home phenomenon," as I have called it, seems to have had its beginning with the confluence of several events. The Eichler family's rental of a home designed by Frank Lloyd Wright had its impact, and Mr. Eichler's relationship with

The Eichler atrium became a well-known feature in many houses built in the late 1950s and afterward. The view to or from this private outdoor environment enhances the spacious feel of the home and often sets a mood for the interior decor.

Accent colors were often used sparingly, in contrast to the main colors of earthen brown, tan, rust, and green.

architect Robert Anshen must have made a major impression. While Mr. Eichler's motives were undoubtedly not altogether altruistic, the sum of all his actions indicates that he strongly wished to create homes of design and taste by using acknowledged architectural talent of the day. He simply had the very good sense not to compromise the use of such talent. That, coupled with his talent and principles, produced what has become a generic term for classic, post-and-beam residential architecture—"an Eichler."

A book of this scope cannot begin to record or capture all of the designs of the Eichler architects. What we hope we have captured, via the photography of Marvin Wax and the book design of Lanning Stern, is the art of the Eichler and its design for living. We hope it will bring back fond memories for former Eichler owners, highlight certain design elements that current owners may now take for granted, and in general provide a tasteful documentation of an era and a phenomenon.

Most Eichler owners will undoubtedly find familiar design elements in many of the photographs, whether from a modestly priced Eichler or from one of the "specials" valued in excess of $1 million. Many of the houses pictured exhibit the classic, clean lines and features of original design and construction. Others illustrate how well the basic architecture accepts tasteful remodeling, which can be achieved by the use of more elegant materials and an appreciation and understanding of the vocabulary spoken by the original design team. All of the homes, and thousands of others not included here, are described well by a statement made by Joseph Eichler in the 1960s: "There are other builders who efficiently produce well-built houses and sell at a fair profit. The purchaser of one of these will get a good value. We believe our houses go beyond this because much more thought and care go into them. Nothing is spent for frills or gimmicks. Beauty is achieved by the architect's skill in designing details, his blend of materials and proper proportions, and above all, the exercise of good taste. In short, we produce a work of art that has gained international reputation."

Indeed it did, and the discussion and appreciation of those accomplishments, and that era, continue to this day, some forty-five years later. We believe our efforts to capture some of that art would be to Mr. Eichler's liking.

Inside, a Wrightian leaded-glass treatment with translucent shell gives a lovely light to the adjacent contrasting textures of concrete block, glass, and wood.

The transition of space, from inside to outside in the traditional home, virtually disappears in the open architecture of the classic Eichler design.

A flat roof line interrupted by a steeply pitched gable roof
segment not only forms an interesting geometric shape, but
also provides a striking shelter for an interesting entry court.

The
West's
lingering
frontier freedom from tradition
also implied social freedom,
which became identified
with living
in a
Modern house
with an
"open plan"
and glass walls
that seemed to bring the
outdoors inside.

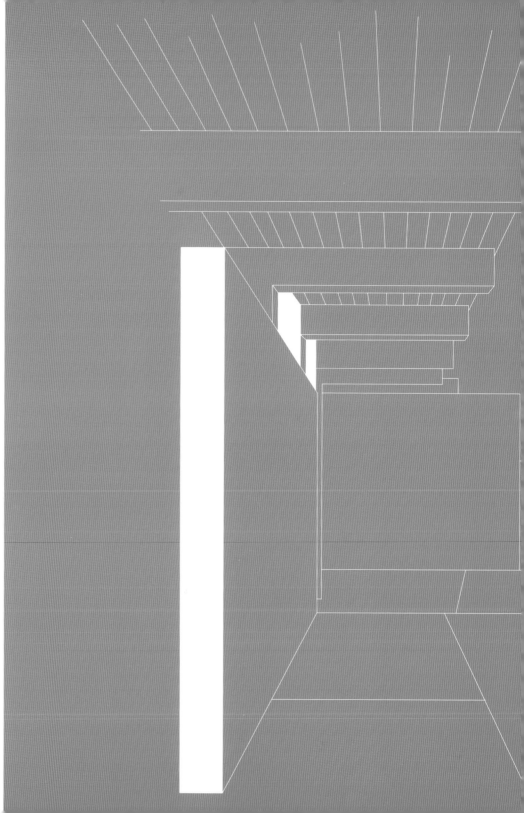

Introduction
Sally B. Woodbridge

An Eichler built home in the late 1940s. A precursor to the homes designed by Anshen & Allen, Jones & Emmons, and later Claude Oakland & Associates. (Photo courtesy, Sally B. Woodbridge.)

"You can get out of my house right now, just get out, you don't deserve to have one of my houses." Do these sound like the words of a man in the business of building and selling houses? Not much. Yet, when Joseph Eichler spoke these words he was soon to become one of the most successful and famous homebuilders of the post–World War II era.

What caused this outburst? James San Jule, Eichler Homes' marketing director from 1949 until 1954, told the story. In the early years Eichler and San Jule regularly spent Sundays—the busiest shopping day in the real estate market—assisting the salesmen in their subdivisions. One Sunday San Jule heard Joe's gravelly voice booming forth from the living room of the model home that both men were showing to a couple. Joe was responding to a question asked by the wife as she pointed to cracks in the beams of the living room ceiling and asked if they were a sign that the house was falling down. An innocent remark no doubt, but to Eichler it indicated ignorance—exposed beams in wood construction usually had cracks that developed as the wood aged—and an unpardonable lack of faith in his product. "He was so proud of his houses," San Jule said, "and besides, he had a short fuse."

Rare photo of Joseph Eichler with all four of the original architectural team. Taken at the Fairmont Hotel in 1952 at an awards luncheon for Eichler Homes. From left to right: Joe Eichler; William Wurster, Dean of the School of Architecture at the University of California at Berkeley; unidentified; Robert Anshen; A. Quincy Jones; Steven Allen; and Frederick Emmons. Claude Oakland, the third architect to be employed by Eichler, joined the team later. (Photo courtesy, James San Jule.)

Although Eichler was a member of the generation of builders who rode the post–World War II housing wave, he was not a typical "merchant builder," as the speculative builders of subdivisions were called. Whereas most merchant builders took pride in their profits and considered design an unnecessary and expensive frill, Eichler was as proud of the design of his houses as he was of his financial success.

What was it about the design of Eichler Homes that gave Joe Eichler such pride? Mainly it was their "custom-designed" appearance: they looked like houses built for the personal clients of reputable architects. They looked that way because the architects who designed them also designed buildings for individual clients, winning awards for themselves and for Eichler Homes. The architects that Eichler employed—Anshen & Allen in San Francisco and Jones & Emmons in Los Angeles—were young and talented. Since merchant builders customarily did not hire licensed professionals to design houses, the industry was virtually closed to architects. But in the late 1940s, the returning war veterans' huge demand for new houses (for which they could obtain very low interest mortgages from the Federal Housing Administration and the Veteran's Administration) enabled many architects to open an office. Nonetheless the opportunity to design for a builder like Joseph Eichler, whose goals included design of the highest quality, was rare. Moreover, while his competitors continued the standard practice of using the services of site-planning engineers, Eichler had his architects design the site plans for his subdivisions. The use of Anshen & Allen's "concentric circle" or "bull's-eye" site plan and Jones & Emmons'

An entry courtyard behind the entry door and concrete block
wall became another outdoor living space adjacent to the sliding
glass doored, all purpose room and kitchen.

The architects' site planning and overall tract layout was an early distinguishing mark of Eichler's home-building style. The gentle, flowing lines of the sidewalks, streets, and landscaping provide a pleasing contrast to the horizontal and vertical design elements of the houses.

"greenbelt scheme"—both of which featured cul-de-sac streets that reduced vehicular traffic—guaranteed that Eichler Homes subdivisions were easily identified on maps. The architects contended that curved streets also created varied views of the houses and more privacy.

Eichler Homes had such innovative features as two bathrooms for three bedroom houses instead of the single bathroom that was the norm in subdivisions across the country. Eichler had suggested to San Jule that, since their houses had radiant heat from pipes in the concrete slab floors, they investigate the costs of having an outdoor patio with radiant heat so that even in the cool of the evening—and summers were cool in coastal California where Eichler was building—people would be able to enjoy outdoor living. While researching these costs, San Jule thought of comparing them to the cost of adding a bathroom, which seemed a much more useful amenity. When the costs turned out to be comparable, Eichler chose the second bath and made history. After Eichler Homes made second baths a standard element, other builders had to follow suit in order to sell their houses. A later innovation, the atrium or interior court, became one of Eichler's favorite features and a hallmark of Eichler Homes.

For whom were Eichler's innovations desirable? Certainly for the young generation of homeowners in the expansionist postwar world who embraced modernity as their lifestyle. Influential books such as the New York Museum of Modern Art's 1946 publication, *If You Want to Build a House,* written by Elizabeth B. Mock, promoted modern living with Modern design. Mock observed, "Light and space work together upon the human psyche, and they have much more to do with our feeling of well-being than is generally granted." Mock went on to state, "The advantages of freedom in space and generous uniform light are peculiar to modern architecture." Numerous books and publications on the Modern house, its furnishings (which were designed not to obstruct one's view by being too massive or too high), and its landscaping reiterated this theme.

The kind of modern living exemplified in Eichler's houses was closely associated with California's famous coastal climate—neither too hot nor too cold, and dry enough so that insects did not force screening of outdoor areas. The West's lingering frontier freedom from tradition also implied social freedom, which became identified with living in a Modern house with an "open plan" and glass walls that seemed to bring the outdoors inside.

Behind this hyperbole lay the reality that fewer interior walls and the use of glass for some exterior walls made these modest structures, ranging from 650 to 800 square feet to 1,500 square feet, seem more spacious. For, although mortgage money was cheap and available, young families did not have large incomes with which to build more space. Besides, their children were typically very young and did not require much personal space. Houses were made to seem larger in floor plans drawn without walls, so that, for example, the children might have a play space in the yard furnished with storage for toys, which looked like a seamless extension of their room. The parents' bedroom might also have an outside space with exercise equipment and lounge furniture. Outdoor counterparts for other indoor spaces became part of the house.

Walls of glass to further the illusion of free-flowing space were facilitated by a system of construction called "post-and-beam." Traditional walls had wood studs placed two feet apart; windows were framed into the wall; and some kind of cladding was put on the exterior, with lath and plaster on the interior. In post-and-beam construction, posts were spaced three to six feet apart—the width varied depending on the weight of the roof material and the strength

of the beams. The downward pressure of the roof was concentrated on beams supported by posts rather than continuously on the walls. When painted white, the modular rhythm of this exposed structure gave a clean, orderly, and open character to the house. The system permitted flexibility in respect to the material used between the supports and thus made glass walls possible. Low-pitched gable roofs or shed roofs enforced the horizontality of the house and furthered the feeling that the roof sheltered the land around it.

Joe Eichler had discovered post-and-beam construction early in his career. In 1947, while perusing the publications about the postwar house and surveying homebuilding activity in the San Francisco Bay Area, he came across the subdivisions of Earl Smith in Richmond. Smith had started out by building housing for wartime shipyard workers. His houses had a concrete slab foundation at ground level and walls constructed according to the post-and-beam system. Their most prominent feature was their unconventional flat roofs. Smith built so many flat-roofed houses in the Bay Area—he became one of the country's biggest homebuilders in the early postwar years—that he became known as "Flat-top" Smith. Eichler bought a set of plans from Smith for

Wide roof overhangs, creating
inviting and handsome entries,
also provide shelter from the
California sun and winter rains.

One of only two, two-story Anshen & Allen designs built in the late 1950s, this lovely home retains the classic interior feel of warm mahogany paneling, redwood washed stain ceiling, and dark structural, post-and-beam members.

$25 with which he built two houses with two bedrooms and a two-car garage; the sale price was $6,800. The houses were on about twenty acres of orchard land in Sunnyvale. Eichler had acquired the land on the advice of Jack Harlow, the construction manager of a firm that sold prefabricated frames for houses, which Eichler had helped finance. Knowing that Eichler wished to become a builder, Harlow took him to see the property and then introduced him to a real estate broker in Sunnyvale. By the end of the day Eichler had purchased the property.

Not wholly satisfied with "Flat-top" Smith's plans, Eichler hired other designers and began reading architectural magazines. In the back of his mind was the fond memory of a house that he and his wife had rented in Hillsborough on the San Francisco peninsula. Frank Lloyd Wright had designed the house, and although Joe had never been interested in architecture, he admired the house and appreciated the architect's skill in making it so special. It was during their stay in the house that the wholesale dairy and poultry products company that Eichler worked for was sold, leaving him with money but nothing to do.

The round landscaping elements present a pleasing contrast to the square stepping path and rectangular entry lines of this flat-roofed home.

"I used to sit around that house," he said, "wondering what I was going to do next. I admired Wright's rich design, with its wooden walls and beamed ceiling, and I asked myself if such houses could be built for ordinary people." This became Eichler's ambition. It was the issue he most wanted to discuss with architect Robert Anshen and Anshen's friend, James San Jule, whom he had invited to Sunnyvale for a discussion of the whys and wherefores of homebuilding. This discussion began one afternoon in 1949 and lasted for three days. It ended with Joe calling in a lawyer to draw up an agreement establishing a corporation with Eichler as principal partner, Anshen as the company architect, and San Jule as the marketing director. Jack Harlow became construction manager for the company, which was called Eichler Homes, Inc.

The rest, as they say, is history. In an interview that the author conducted in 1972 with Proctor Melquist, longtime editor of that bible of western homemakers, *Sunset* magazine, he stated that a 1950s poll of their readers had shown that over 60 percent of them owned Eichler homes. During these boom years Eichler devoted more and more time to interpreting the public's preferences in colors and amenities. He viewed his houses as expressions of the American Dream, a belief that

Architects, designers, and other professionals associated with the visual arts were often buyers of the early Eichlers. That is still the case today. The open space and varied ceiling heights provide a fitting setting for artwork of all varieties.

was strengthened by the news that some buyers even named their babies after him.

Today, an Eichler home is still a valid image of the American dream house, which is more an image, alas, than an attainable reality. Joe Eichler's great personal integrity and commitment to the highest standards of design have insured that his name has a place in history that is equal to that of many of the country's outstanding architects—a great achievement for a "merchant builder."

By the mid 1950s
virtually every
Bay Area resident

could recognize
and even describe
an "Eichler,"

for good
or for ill,

which is
something

no other
homebuilder

has ever
accomplished.

A Cherished Legacy
Ned Eichler

The low-pitched gable roof of the Eichler home was employed at one time or another by all of the Eichler architectural firms—Anshen & Allen, Jones & Emmons, and Claude Oakland & Associates.

I was seventeen and a freshman in college when my father became a builder. During summer vacations I worked for him driving a truck, installing lawns, "laying out" for a framing crew, and learning how to estimate and buy materials. After two years in the army, I managed marketing for Eichler Homes and helped the company reach its apex in the late 1950s. In 1961 my father made the fateful decision to diversify into central-city, high-rise apartment construction. I opposed this decision, and after getting into a classic father-and-son power fight over the direction of the company, I left the business.

Over the thirty or so years since my resignation, I have done many things—taught in three universities, written several books about real estate, was vice-president of a national apartment building company, managed the disposition of the massive real estate holdings of the bankrupt Penn Central railroad, and ironically, was president of Levitt and Sons, the other postwar homebuilding company to achieve lasting fame. In 1980 I returned to the University of California to teach for a year and write a history of American merchant building since 1945. During the last eight years, I have founded and run a mortgage banking firm specializing in loans on existing apartments, completed

The striking A-frame roof line of this Jones & Emmons design may have been inspired by steeply pitched roofs of mountain chalets. Its use to dramatize the entry, atrium, and living room worked equally well in the climate of sunny California.

The long, low horizontal lines of this classic Eichler design by Jones & Emmons form a perfect framework for the almost mysterious Asian feel of this atrium.

the required courses for a Ph.D. in history, and written *The Thrift Debacle,* a depiction and analysis of the savings and loans and savings banks since their inception in the early 1800s.

In all this time I have never written about the personalities of the top builders and developers I have known. More importantly—at least to me—I have not publicly given my father the credit he deserves. As his son, as one who knew him and his achievements intimately, and as a writer, I have decided it is time to share what I know about a group of men among whom only my father was truly singular.

Joseph L. Eichler was born in 1900. His father was a gentle, diminutive, Austrian-Jewish immigrant who owned a small toy store on 57th Street and Second Avenue in New York, but who preferred playing his violin over running the shop. My grandmother, a German Jew, was a powerful woman who led the business and the family—there was a younger brother and sister—until she died in 1916. My father worshiped her and was devastated by her death. He attended New York University, an experience he always described fondly, often recounting specific courses and professors. After receiving a business degree in 1920, he had a series of unsatisfactory jobs assisting investment advisers. In 1925 he married the daughter of Polish-Jewish immigrants who had gained considerable success in a wholesale butter and egg business. Their "mixed" marriage was unusual: she, the East European Jew, came from a rich family, and he, the German-Austrian, did not. My parents' common bond was a zealous commitment to modernity.

The Eichlers moved to San Francisco, where my father was employed by the West Coast branch of my mother's family business. For the next twenty years, though he performed well and was highly respected as the company's chief financial officer, Joe Eichler hated his job. He was working for someone else, and the work was uninspiring. However, because he made a very good living in the middle of the Great Depression and because he never revealed his deepest feelings, he persevered in apparently good spirits. In 1927 Richard, my older brother, was born. I, the second and only other child, arrived in 1930.

America abounds with stories of Jews, even very poor ones, especially those like my parents who were born here, immersing themselves in the arts, philosophy, and political theory. This was not true of our family. My mother's consuming interests

A near abstraction can be found in the horizontal and vertical lines of shoji sliding doors abutting the frosted and clear glass ceiling panes.

The Eichler Atrium: Outdoor environment and space captured for living.

44

Posts-and-beams, their juxtaposition with one another, and their varied in-fill panel options, provided the architects with a long-proven construction system upon which to base their many home designs. Here, beams that extend beyond the interior space, on top of posts, and hidden within walls and siding, also perform an exterior design function, supporting the arbor-like cross members.

were clothes, her golf club, and having drinks and dinner with club friends, after which cards were played. In 1936, we moved from a modest San Francisco flat to an equally modest suburban San Mateo home—bought for about $9,000 with three mortgages—of nondescript design and traditionally furnished. The one manifestation of culture was my father's reading of some contemporary prose fiction—Hemingway, Fitzgerald, Steinbeck, and Dreiser, for example. And yet he never read Joyce, Faulkner, Lawrence, Dickens, Hardy, Melville, or Twain, among others. They owned no classical records and only listened to pop on the radio. My parents never attended the opera, the ballet, or the symphony, nor, until at least the late 1940s, did they go to an art gallery. My father occasionally quoted Shakespeare—"sufficient unto the day..."—but none of the Bard's works was ever in our house. He also often sang bits of Gilbert and Sullivan.

Despite this near absence of interests in the arts, Joe Eichler manifested a certain aesthetic sense. The clearest example was the way he dressed. He bought his clothes—suits and sport coats were often custom-made—and composed his outfits with great care. The manner was conservative— Brooks Brothers' cuts—but he had a decided flair.

Opposite: The simple, plain facades of these Jones & Emmons designs gives a clear illustration of the influence of the International Style on the Eichler architects.

A community center was an innovative and distinguishing feature of several Eichler developments. The site plan drawn here included a three acre park with a 60x30 pool, completely equipped playground, and two major buildings for use as a nursery school and meeting hall. The center was planned by a well-known landscape architect, Thomas Church, and designed by Jones & Emmons.

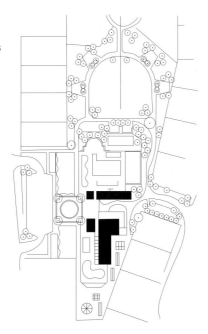

His model was Fred Astaire. He might have worn a tan gabardine suit with a bright blue silk tie, matching blue socks and breast pocket handkerchief, and brown suede shoes. He was an avid golfer but never wore resort clothes, such as bright, multicolored slacks and pale red or blue blazers. Even when just hanging around the house on weekends—a rare occurrence anyway—he never put on jeans, corduroys, or the like. His idea of casual dress was gray slacks with a subdued checked sport shirt and a navy sport coat. Except when playing golf in the rain, he never wore a zippered jacket.

In one other way my father evidenced a deep feeling for physical style. He greatly admired athletes and dancers who were not merely successful but graceful, who performed well without apparent effort. Again, Astaire was his idol. In sports it was Bobby Jones, not just because he won but because his swing was so smooth, and Joe DiMaggio: "If you ever get to see him play center field," my father once urged me, "watch him go after a fly ball hit seemingly out of reach. He'll start running as the bat touches the ball, even before. His strides will be long and without a break, and he'll be waiting when the ball comes down.

The wonderful thing is that he makes catches no one else could get close to, and he makes them look so easy." Ten years later, when the Yankee Clipper had a bad foot and was nearing the end of his career, I saw him play in Fenway Park. Hobbled as he was, DiMaggio made a catch exactly as my father had described. He also went four for four and when he was substituted after his last hit, the partisan Boston crowd gave the tired DiMaggio a thunderous ovation. Expressionless and limp, he trotted to the dugout with unmistakable elegance. I remembered my father's words.

My father was not particularly handsome. He was of average height and weight—5'9", 160 pounds—and not himself very graceful physically. He started losing his hair early and was nearly bald by the time he turned forty. He was very nearsighted, wore thick glasses, and had a large and substantially hooked nose. In addition, he was an inveterate smoker of cigars, which he chewed prodigiously. Though as far as I know he never committed infidelity, he was attractive to, and interested in, many women. One reason was his wonderful sense of humor, which was often sardonic but stopped just short of being harsh or malicious, and which he turned on himself at least as often as on others. He treated women in most

Cork flooring and either redwood or mahogany paneling of the early 1950s homes have often been replaced by many different kinds of floor materials, including wood parquet, and brightened wall surfaces using textured wallpaper or paint.

Opposite page: An early 1950s Anshen & Allen design, and a precursor to the model inspiring the enormously successful atrium design.

Thermador appliances, Zolatone treated kitchen cabinetry with sliding doors, and the familiar extendable, swing-out table. While Eichler kitchens are often the focus of upgrades and remolding, the simple beauty and functional capacity of this 1950s kitchen remains to this day.

Opened space from open beamed post-and-beam construction allows a virtually boundless space with which to express one's personal vision.

respects as he treated men, including them in his barbs but also implicitly assuming they were capable of intelligent conversation. Still, he was captivated by female beauty. Leaving a movie starring Rita Hayworth, he turned to me and said, "What a dish." And when I was fourteen, as we were walking together in San Francisco, he jabbed my arm asking, "Did you see her?" Sheepishly I said I had not. "Good God," he roared, "what kind of a kid am I raising?" No small part of his affection for my mother lay in her looks—she was beautiful and dressed with style.

With apparently no previous interest in architecture, painting, sculpture, or even decoration, my father came home one night in 1942 and announced that we were moving immediately—to a rented house designed by Frank Lloyd Wright. Our stay in the Wright house was temporary. The owner returned after a few years, and we had to move. It was clear, however, that my parents had become devotees of contemporary architecture: my father because it tapped some buried aesthetic yearning, and both of them because of their dislike of the traditional. So they bought a lot and hired a young Wright disciple, Robert Anshen, to design a house for them. Since their limited budget could not meet their extravagant demands, the project

The strategic placement of the abbreviated low-pitched gable roof on the otherwise long horizontal wall of wood, brick, and glass creates a dramatic entry to this Claude Oakland design.

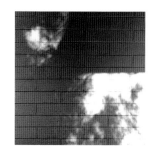

never came to fruition. (Not until 1951, four years after my father had become a builder, did they finally move into a house Anshen designed for them.) In 1945 we left the Wright house and occupied two rooms in a nearby country club. Almost a year later we moved again, to a modest, two-bedroom apartment in a small San Francisco building my father bought as an investment.

While all this residential turmoil was going on, the family business was sold. My father did not remain with the company, but neither his energy nor the family's spending habits permitted retirement. At the age of forty-five, he was finally liberated from unsatisfying toil, but he had no idea what to do next. For about a year he played golf and explored alternatives. As word got around that he was seeking investments and/or involvement, two young engineers asked him for financial help. They had recently started a business in Sunnyvale—prefabricating small houses to be built on one's lot. After putting up a few thousand dollars, my father decided that his "partners" could use his financial and accounting skills. He began spending two days a week at their office. Soon, however, exasperated with their unbusinesslike manner, he bought them out.

Another modest entry facade belies the magnificent treatment
of the interior space in this home.

A year or so later, a real estate broker acquaintance approached my father. "Joe," he said, "you can't get anywhere doing this. Why don't you build a tract?" "Where the hell would I get the land, or the money?" my father demanded. Of course, the broker just happened to have the property, fifty lots in east Sunnyvale, and my father found a bank to fund the project. One of the two most famous postwar homebuilding companies, Eichler Homes, was launched. The other company was Levitt and Sons.

Contrary to the accepted notion, Joe Eichler made no immediate connection between his interest in Wright-style modern architecture and building homes for sale. His first tract houses in 1947 sold for $10,000 and were conventional—wood floors on joists, sheet-rock walls, forced air heat, and so on. He did introduce minor design advancements in certain finish work—such as cabinets and light fixtures—but the conception of the early projects remained traditional. Late in 1948, however, Bob Anshen brought my father's two worlds together. Anshen's attempt to design an acceptable and affordable Eichler family home had continued. At the end of one of a long series of meetings to review the latest plan, Anshen and my father stood outside looking at the latest tract my father had

The wall containing the range-top and built-in barbecue also acts as a room/space divider in this beautifully remodeled kitchen.

under construction (one house had been temporarily
converted into an office). Anshen, like a character
out of Dickens—small body, enormous head,
always dressed in a dark gray flannel suit and vest,
red or black knit tie, and white socks—patterned
not only his designs but his manner after Frank
Lloyd Wright. "Joe," he blurted out in a voice as
loud as my father's, "How can someone like you,
who loves real architecture, build this crap? Why
don't you let me do some houses for you?" My
father was appalled and said, "For Christ's sake,
Bob, you can't even conceive a house for me I can
build for $100,000. I sell these things, with a lot,
for $10,000." Anshen snapped back, "Your house
hasn't got a goddamned thing to do with it. You and
your wife make it expensive. These are production
houses and I can design them. Pay me $2,500 for
three plans and I'll show you." My father, as always
chewing on his cigar, stared darkly at Anshen for a
moment and walked toward his office. As he got to
the door, without turning around or removing the
cigar from his mouth, he said two words, "Do it."

On a dusty, unfinished street in Sunnyvale what has
been known ever since as an "Eichler" was born.

Gray, quarry tiled floors are used throughout the living and dining room areas in this clerestoried windowed Jones & Emmons design. Sliding shoji panels can separate the areas from one another if one chooses.

Anshen delivered—three-bedroom, one-bath, nine-hundred-square-foot houses with redwood siding, paneling, and post-and-beam ceilings, floor-to-ceiling glass on the rear facade, open-interior planning, and radiant-heated concrete floors, fifty of which were built and sold for $9,500. When the model homes were opened, they evoked enormous interest both from the media and from prospective buyers, many of whom worked in Palo Alto and could afford considerably more expensive homes. One Sunday, as my father stood outside the models proudly observing the crowds and the sales activity, the same broker who had sold him the first subdivision lots walked over, put his arm around his shoulders, and warned him, "Joe, you can't do this. These houses will never sell." My father looked at him, pointed at the people signing contracts, and shot back, "You dumb son-of-a-bitch; what the hell do you think they're doing?"

These first Anshen designs in 1949 were the basis for over ten thousand houses built during the next eighteen years. Naturally, there were many refinements, and considerable upgrading—a second or even third bath, a family room, a fourth bedroom, an atrium, "split" plan (the master bedroom and a study on one side and three bedrooms

While one seldom, if ever, thinks of Eichler architecture as a fitting start for Spanish or Southwest redesign, its open space can provide a palette or framework for the creative architect and interior designer.

A. QUINCY JON

AREA ANALYSIS   EMIEL BECSKY   ASSOCIATES   ARCHITECTS & SITE PLANNERS
                 HARRY SAUNDERS   MEMBERS OF THE AMERICAN INSTITUTE OF ARCHITECTS
                 KAZ NOMURA   12248 SANTA MONICA BLVD.
                 LOUIS LILTS   LOS ANGELES 25, CALIFORNIA
                 WILLIAM LAFFIN   PHONE: BRADSHAW 2-8208
                 JOHN THOMAN

FLOOR PLAN

EICHLER HOMES   SJ 1504   1 OF 8

and a bath on the other), peaked roofs, more sliding doors, laundry areas in the bedroom wing, and so on. But the basic theme remained—blank front facades, rear and sometimes side walls of floor-to-ceiling glass, fenced yards, kitchens open to the family room, wood siding and post-and-beam ceilings, both stained, and radiant-heated concrete floors. There were also some early innovations in subdivision planning—a tract with streets in concentric circles, community clubhouses and swimming pools, and a group of attached town houses. All of these were firsts in the industry but were not generally continued. The defining characteristic of Eichler Homes was the design of the house.

By the mid 1950s virtually every Bay Area resident could recognize and even describe an "Eichler," for good or for ill, which is something no other homebuilder has ever accomplished. Annual production was raised from under a hundred units in Sunnyvale to over nine hundred in 1955, the company's peak year, when operations had been expanded to Palo Alto, San Mateo, Walnut Creek, San Rafael, and Sacramento. By this time Eichler Homes had been featured not only in virtually every local newspaper and magazine but in national publications such as *Life, Architectural Forum,* and

Hillside lots provided a
change of pace for
Eichler's architects and
construction team. The
horizontal planes of this
home and its exterior
space travel up and
down the configuration
of this lot.

House and Garden and in architectural journals throughout the world. In 1959, Eichler Homes sold its stock to the public (three months before Levitt and Sons), the first American homebuilder to do so. A year later there was further geographic expansion, to Southern California. Finally, in 1961, site acquisition and planning began for several projects in San Francisco, principally high-rise apartment buildings, whose eventual cost overruns and market deficiencies would hopelessly overwhelm the company's financial resources. Despite all this diversification, which included construction of San Francisco's most famous and prestigious apartment building, The Summit on Russian Hill, the main legacy of Eichler Homes is generally considered to be the houses built in Sunnyvale, Palo Alto, and San Rafael.

Few people realize how superbly Eichler Homes organized its production. Joe Eichler was responsible for this, as for every other important aspect of the company. He had no technical training, previous building experience, or even a tinkerer's interest. He had never held a hammer, a saw, or a wrench in his hand, before and even after 1947. Still, he became a master builder, in one respect more than his East Coast counterpart, Bill Levitt, or any other builder. All of the large-scale, postwar

The rather unassuming facade of this Jones & Emmons design, as with countless other Eichlers, prompts the street-side observer to ponder what the interior looks like.

Inside the visitor is greeted
first by an entry atrium
always patterned by
abstract shadows, and then
a tastefully redesigned
open interior.

The open space of the Eichler invited even further opening in this tastefully redesigned interior. Concrete slab flooring enables a wide choice of flooring materials, including a handsome slate.

homebuilders steamlined the process of building through labor specialization, product standardization, and vastly improved supply planning and organization. Many of them, like my father and Levitt (a lawyer), had no previous experience in the field. All of them, except my father, simplified house designs to facilitate production. They despised and avoided architects, who espoused and tried to impose architectural principles that complicated construction. My father, on the other hand, embraced them, hiring first Anshen and later A. Quincy Jones, two highly respected young advocates of modern architecture. He therefore set for himself the task of organizing the efficient production of structures whose detailing and materials were complex and unfamiliar to suppliers, subcontractors, and directly employed craftsmen.

A full description of the difficulties in mass producing Eichler Homes so that they could be offered at a marketable price and delivered on a predictable schedule would require hundreds of pages. I shall give only a few examples. The use of wood interior paneling presented several problems. Redwood plywood was available and, while more costly than sheet rock, not too expensive. However, it had two defects: it was very soft and it was very dark. Lighter Philippine mahogany would have

The Eichler atrium is often a perfect environment for lush tropical plants. The atrium pictured here utilizes additional horizontal members for further shielding from the sun.

Zolotone painted surfaces on kitchen cabinetry have been replaced by a variety of materials from Formica, seen here, to elegant woods, to brushed aluminum. The familiar flecked Formica used on earlier horizontal surfaces has been replaced with an even greater variety of new surfaces; granite, seen here, as well as marble, tile, and synthetic stone, such as Corian, can now be found in remodeled Eichler kitchens.

One of two prototype steel-frame homes built by Eichler, this Jones & Emmons design, dubbed "the X-100," provides yet another example of Eichler's tendency to be at the forefront of residential building. Had the concept of living in the steel-frame home been accepted by the American public and construction costs been contained, Eichler would undoubtedly have been one of the earliest steel-frame builders.

been better, but although it was the cheapest hardwood, it was still expensive and difficult to obtain at a consistent quality level. After fits and starts, we were able to get manufacturers to buy logs in the Philippines, import them to Japan, make plywood to our specifications, and ship it to the United States at a satisfactory price. For several years Eichler Homes was one of the largest American users of this product.

Modern architecture held that, as much as possible, the inherent structure of a house should be visible, and the walls facing nature (in this case rear yards) should provide minimal visual obstruction—"bring the outdoors in." Thus, in an Eichler Home the roof was constructed with widely spaced beams (six to eight feet) carrying roof decking (two-inch boards). In garden walls the beams sat on posts, which in turn sat on footings under the concrete slab. Between the posts were glass panels or sliding glass doors, which sat on sills and were held in place by small pieces of wood called "stops." It would have been far easier and cheaper to have the beams closer together so the roof decking could be thinner and so that plate glass would not be required. The beams could have been smaller, cheaper, and easier to handle if a "header" were placed in the glass wall underneath beams running

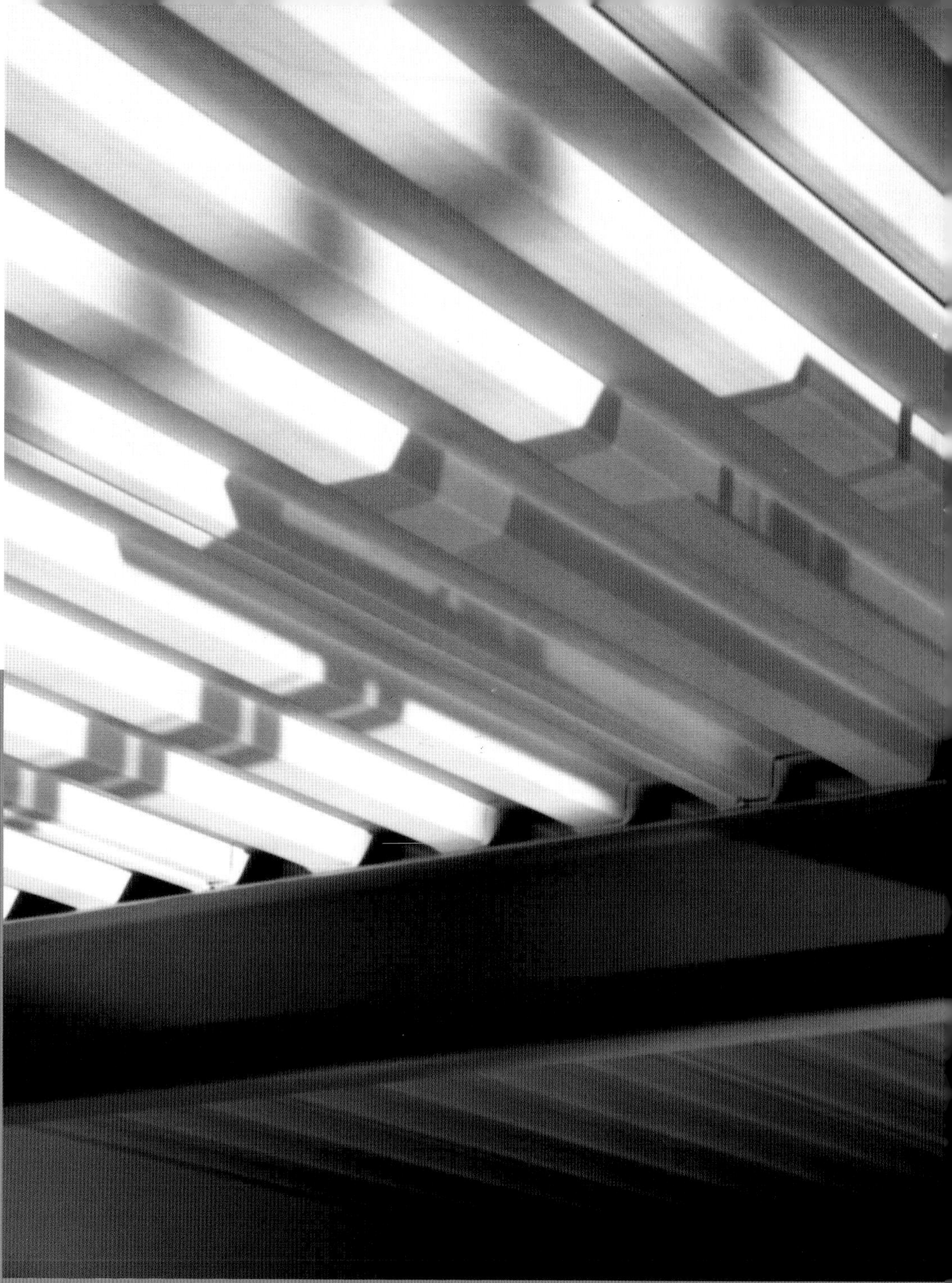

to the outside. However, by making construction easier and less costly, architectural principles my father had come to hold dear would have been violated.

Throughout the life of the company there were frequent design meetings in which construction and sales people pleaded with him and the architects to make the houses easier to build and/or to sell. Sometimes, of course, he acceded. But he did so grudgingly and only after tenacious resistance. The architects were often less "principled" than he. I can still see my father in those meetings, pilloried by everyone, including me, and finally yelling, "Enough, we'll keep doing it right." It was this incredible integrity that endeared him to the architects who worked for him and to the profession in general. Forced to serve philistines, architects saw him, even when they disagreed with his taste, as uniquely honest. They were right. Much as the construction superintendents sometimes thought he was nuts, they too respected him for standing his ground.

Anshen and my father often fought, sometimes almost like lovers. After one such yelling match in 1953—a dispute about money—they got a divorce (A. Q. Jones was hired to substitute). Anshen then

Open entry skylights,
an open door, and open
space for living.

committed an unforgivable sin: he offered his services to our closest competitor, who apparently concluded he could successfully build and sell a modified version of an Eichler Home. My father was infuriated but also curious about what the offspring of these apparently incompatible bedfellows would look like.

It was standard practice for builders, my father included, to visit competitive projects with their top sales and construction managers. Upon hearing the new Anshen models were nearing completion, he took his entourage to see them. What he beheld was nearly every corruption of "good architecture"—windows out of line, a jumble of different materials, and so on—that he and presumably Anshen cherished. Then he spotted Anshen, who was on site for a design review meeting, and called him over. Pointing at the models, he bellowed in outrage, "Bob, you son-of-a-bitch, look at this. It has every goddamn phony trick people wanted me to use and you argued against. How can you design this crap for these people?" Anshen, who had listened to this diatribe patiently and with a slight smile on his face, broke into laughter. "Joe," he said, "they don't know any better. But you do. You understand what architecture is all about and you know what's

A fireplace, open on two sides, becomes both a focal point and space divider in this Claude Oakland design. Large skylights over one area further define and even prompt a different mood from the other.

right. I can do this junk for them. I could never do it for you. And you wouldn't let me." My father glared at him for a long time, and then his face melted into a broad grin. Soon Anshen abandoned his new client and was once more designing Eichler Homes.

As the 1950s wore on, other builders occasionally tried to capture a share of Eichler Homes' market by building a softened version. They believed that, while my father's product had substantial appeal to young families with upper-middle-class taste but lower-middle-class incomes, his strict adherence to principle was too limiting. None of their efforts succeeded. Most observers at the time, or later, assumed incorrectly that the main cause lay in weak sales. However, the emulators' difficulties were in construction. So efficient had our company become by 1955 that, despite the relatively high cost of so many materials used in an Eichler Home and our requirement for skilled workmen, especially carpenters, we could build a house with at least equivalent features at the same square-foot cost as those building conventional houses. Even people who had serious reservations about some of the visual aspects of an Eichler Home bought them anyway because of their floor plans and basic value.

Classic furniture designed by the icons of an era—
Eames, Nelson, Saarinen, and Bertoia—was used
by the Eichler design team in model homes, and it
remains a perfect complement to the classic lines
of Eichler architecture.

Joe Eichler was determined that his houses be both architecturally sound and marketable. No construction difficulty was too small to get his attention, nor was it, for him, intractable. Larry Weinberg, financially the most successful postwar merchant builder, once asked me, "Why does your father make life so hard for himself? He is an organizational and marketing genius, but those damn houses are too tough for real production. He could make a lot more money if he changed the designs." There was no way to respond. Larry had one frame of reference—maximum profit. My father had another. To continue operating, he also had to make money; having it enabled him to live well and, as I shall explain below, support certain causes. But building houses was a vehicle for his personal aesthetic, even artistic, expression. He infused employees, subcontractors, and suppliers with his zeal, and for a decade or so, together they performed a near miracle.

Inevitably, working through many other people and being restrained by zoning laws, building codes, bankers, the weather, business slumps, and the like often frustrated my father's creative impulses. He was not in the same position as a poet, novelist, painter, or composer. He came closest to having their freedom in one activity at

The vast majority of Eichler residences were separate homes built on individual lots, yet the Eichler organization also designed and constructed adjoining row houses, cooperatives, and condominium units. Regardless of house type, every interior had the distinct Eichler ambiance, often accented by the atrium.

Eichler Homes. Without anyone quite noticing, my father began not only to choose house colors but to invent his own. There he would be, out on a construction job, impeccably dressed as always, studying a piece of scrap wood on which the painter had tried out his latest composition. Soon he had a small outside area set up at home where he experimented with mixtures, many of which became standard manufacturer colors. Even the architects began asking his advice on the subject for their own projects.

While he had more control over colors than any other visual aspect of an Eichler Home, even that was not total. Customers had their own ideas and often rebelled against Joe Eichler designating how the exterior of the home they were buying should be stained. He compromised by assigning two or three colors to each house and then allowing the purchaser to choose, but he kept a sharp eye out for resultant combinations of colors of which he disapproved. Once he was driving by a house being painted and jumped out of the car. "Who the hell picked this color?" he demanded. "The buyer," a painter told him. "It doesn't go right with the houses on either side. Change it." "But Joe," the painter said, "the owners were just here and they really want this color. After all, it's their house."

The influence of the Bauhaus schools of art and architecture upon the exterior design of these homes seems evident. Inside, they are quintessential Eichler.

The golden, rolling, oak studded hills of the California landscape provide a fitting backdrop for this Jones & Emmons design.

"Like hell it is," my father told him. "It's my house. Change the goddamn color."

One of the persisting misconceptions about Eichler Homes surrounds the introduction and significance of the "atrium." Its origin and evolution illustrate the way the company handled design, my father's crucial role, and how rarely anyone could foresee outcomes. By 1957 most Eichler Homes had four bedrooms, two baths, and a family room. There were three or four different arrangements of the spaces, or models, and two or three lines, mainly differentiated by size. Prices ranged from $18,000 to $25,000. For us, as for other builders, selling enough houses to sustain volume, make some kind of profit, and most important of all for an undercapitalized company, pay the bills was a daily struggle. From time to time recessions, accompanied by high interest rates, sharply curtailed sales. Everyone tinkered with features, altered advertising, hired new sales people, and offered discounts, but none of it made much difference. As a colorful Texas builder, the late Ike Jacobs, once put it: "When the people meet on the courthouse steps and decide not to buy, there is nothing you can do about it. Running more ads, lowering the price, or raising commissions to boost sales is like pissing into a Texan gale."

The year 1957 fit Ike's description. One of our main tracts was in Palo Alto. Sales were so bad that, as the marketing manager, I fired the on-site salesman and moved my office to the models. I saved some overhead but did not produce more customers. Especially at such times, we had numerous meetings with the architects in a relentless search for more appealing or less expensive houses. On one such occasion, Anshen sketched at least a hundred schemes, none of which struck anyone as promising. The meeting began to break up. We were exhausted and depressed. Anshen continued doodling and shoved a rough plan at my father and me, a house wrapped around a courtyard. We looked at it skeptically. "What the hell is that thing in the middle?" my father asked. "An atrium," Bob answered. "The Romans used to use them." With that, Anshen departed, leaving a sea of scribbles on tracing paper. My father and I later returned to them. There was the atrium, and it made no sense—more exterior walls and therefore more cost, a "boxy" look, a useless courtyard, and so on. So desperate were we to do something, however, that finally we decided to try it. We built four new models, three of them variations of older plans and one Anshen's atrium design. The latter had minimal impact, partly because of the way the house looked from the street and partly because

The typical earthen palette of the original interiors provides a pleasant, warm background for the striking accent colors used so appropriately in this living room.

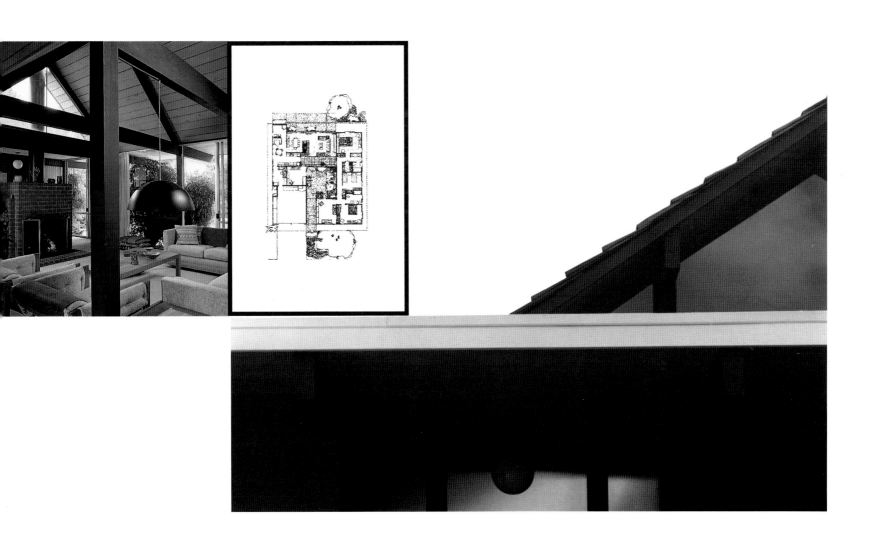

An unassuming facade
and carport entry is a quiet
prelude to interior light and
space, often dramatically
captured with interior decor.

we could propose no logical use of the atrium to prospective buyers.

At a later meeting Quincy Jones studied Anshen's atrium house. "I think it's a great idea," he said, "but it's not quite handled right." Quincy then did his own sketches. By rearranging the plan he found a way to eliminate the boxy look and open the courtyard just enough to make a major difference. We introduced his version just as the sales slump ended. It was an instant success; soon virtually every Eichler Home was built around an atrium. For some time we still did not understand why people were so attracted to this concept. After visiting many owners, we confirmed our original view that the atrium had little practical use. Nevertheless, it had an enormous impact. One of the main criticisms of an Eichler Home had been its minimal and unassuming entry. Inadvertently, we had solved the problem. Now, after approaching a still relatively austere Eichler Home and opening the front door, one was met with a surprise—an enclosed courtyard. Furthermore, one got a wonderful visual experience from the halls surrounding this space. No one foresaw how significant a factor the atrium was to become.

The brushed aluminum cabinetry of this striking kitchen remodel stands in stark but studied contrast to the natural warm colors of the slate flooring and original redwood ceiling.

The home on this and the following three pages beautifully embodies the architectural type and aesthetic achieved by Joseph Eichler and his architects. One not only lives with the beauty of classic design, but with the beauty of nature outside brought inside.

The unaltered redwood ceiling,
mellowed with age, is the perfect
complement to the exposed
aggregate loggia.

The atrium generated myriad construction problems—drainage, more and complicated foundation
structures, special detailing of the front screen,
roof connections, and so on. Production people
hated it and initially fought to get rid of it. But once
more my father's tenacity carried the day. By
1959, all those difficulties had been overcome;
building atrium houses became routine. No other
builder had the ability, the perseverance, the loyalty
of his crews, or the desire to fight the battle.
Winning it solidified the company's position. With
tracts in Sunnyvale, Palo Alto, Walnut Creek, and
San Rafael and the atrium perfected, Eichler
Homes went public (stock sale) in 1959 and began
its heyday.

However, even as the company went public, was
building an average of seven hundred houses a
year, was expanding into Southern California, and
would earn steady though not spectacular profits
from 1959 to 1962, several trends ran against
Eichler Homes. First, those materials and processes
that were peculiar to our product—glass, redwood,
mahogany plywood—were becoming relatively
more expensive and difficult to obtain or install.
Second, especially in areas with higher summer
temperatures like Sunnyvale, San Jose, San
Rafael, and Walnut Creek, buyers were beginning

92

Eichler space seems the perfect repository for furniture designed by the contemporary masters, such as Eero Saarinen. The contrasting antique cabinet appears almost as a realistic painting in this well but softly lighted space.

to want air-conditioning. An Eichler Home with its radiant-heated concrete floor, rear glass walls, post-and-beam ceiling, and built-up roof was virtually impossible to air-condition in any cost-effective way. Third, many of the kinds of people who had previously liked and chosen Eichler Homes had become wealthier and desirous of greater individualization in their homes. Fourth, there was a growing preference for more romantic architecture, often expressed in the purchase and remodeling of older houses. Fifth, other builders had become more sophisticated in designing a product that, while conventional, had some of the attributes associated with an Eichler Home.

I, more than anyone else, pointed these developments out to my father. At least openly, he denied their effects for two very good reasons. First, there were no easy or perhaps even possible solutions. Second, those adaptations that might have mitigated their effects mostly required compromises with his architectural principles. Sensing what was happening, he turned his attention to a new challenge, building central-city, high-rise apartments. Why could he not bring to them the unique combination of skills—an acute feel for design and an ability to organize construction—he had applied with such success to tract housing

The gray-washed stained redwood ceilings were always supported by either white or dark brown/black beams. The earth-tone, gray brick fireplace undoubtedly generated the marvelous color scheme of this home.

Opposite page: Extending the outdoor living space with a post-and-beam arbor beautifully complements this flat roof design.

This page: Houses built in the 1960s and 1970s used less redwood and Philippine mahogany paneling to brighten the interior. The interior of this redecorated home was lightened even further by painting the redwood ceiling and selecting light, finished kitchen cabinetry.

This early Jones & Emmons "split-level" two-story design accommodated a hillside lot by placing the carport and storage area above and the two-story living area on the lower grade. The striking color of the stained exterior has been maintained by the original owner.

fifteen years earlier? Many people, including me, suggested at the time that the analogy seemed fallacious, but who could be sure? After all, had he listened to all the naysayers earlier, an Eichler Home would never have come into being. However, the result was financial disaster, and the company would only survive another five years.

As a homebuilder, Joe Eichler was not only innovative in his approach to architecture. Eichler Homes was the first large, tract builder to sell houses to African-Americans. Geography and the social environment were crucial factors in this. The San Francisco Bay Area was ideal for our houses. Its temperate climate and lush landscaping provided a perfect physical setting. Furthermore, it had a cosmopolitan and liberal atmosphere. In other words, it was easier to build and sell an Eichler Home here than it would have been (or was) anywhere else. In addition, most, though surely not all, Eichler owners were less inclined toward racial or religious prejudice than the Bay Area population as a whole, let alone people in other parts of the country.

Before 1954 we had sold to Asians and built a home for an African-American NAACP official on his own lot. In the middle of that year an African-American woman, a nurse, called me to ask if

This home's roof/ceiling, as well as stairs, were formed by joining massive 2x8 lumber side-by-side, and securing with bolts and adhesive. The durability of such construction will probably be measured by centuries.

A copper tubing pattern, like those used in the radiant heating system of Eichler homes, is seen here in the abstract, sculpture-like, but is functional, heating the space in the two-story entry of this home.

we would sell a house in our latest Palo Alto subdivision to her and her husband, an African-American engineer. There were then no laws on racial discrimination. I told her frankly that I didn't know and asked if we could meet. We did and I learned three facts. First, by any other than a racial standard—income, education, profession—the couple was eminently qualified. Second, while they already knew which model and even which lot they wanted, they had no enthusiasm for the design of an Eichler Home; for them it represented the location they wanted and good value. Third, the wife especially, who had a large chip on her shoulder, would be an extremely difficult person in any dispute, whether with us or other homeowners.

I reported all this to my father. His reaction was mixed and casual. After seeking my opinion—which was that on balance we should do the right thing and sell them a house—he said, "Well, do what you want. If you sell it to them, handle it as carefully as you can." We did so and incurred wrath from a few neighbors before the African-American family took occupancy. The same thing happened the following year in San Rafael. In each case, however, as soon as the African-American family moved in, the furor ended.

The use of concrete block walls and pillar impart a
certain timeless quality to this home designed by
Claude Oakland.

This glassed-in double-A roof line permits a cathedral lighting feel from front to rear, as well as a marvelous elevated "pool" for reflected images.

From then on, I managed a policy under which, without publicly announcing or even discussing the subject, we sold perhaps thirty to forty houses a year to African-Americans. The company was probably hurt financially—mostly by an untraceable loss of sales—but it was never a significant business issue. My father became involved only on rare occasions when groups of homeowners demanded he refrain from completing a sale to an African-American family in their neighborhood. Not so much arguing for racial tolerance, although he strongly believed in it, he responded with outrage that people were trying to bully him. "I am not a fool," he told one such gathering. "If, as you claim, this will destroy property values, I could lose millions. You put up a lousy $500 and get a loan guaranteed by the government. You should be ashamed of yourselves for wasting your time and mine with such pettiness." Most of them sheepishly left the room. A few stayed to complain about an unrepaired warped door or leaking faucet.

My father first became politically active in 1952. He had long been a Democrat and liberal, supporting Henry Wallace, for example. But, as he himself said in 1960, "I got into politics with Stevenson and I'll go out with him." (Actually he continued to be involved throughout the 1960s.) Even in

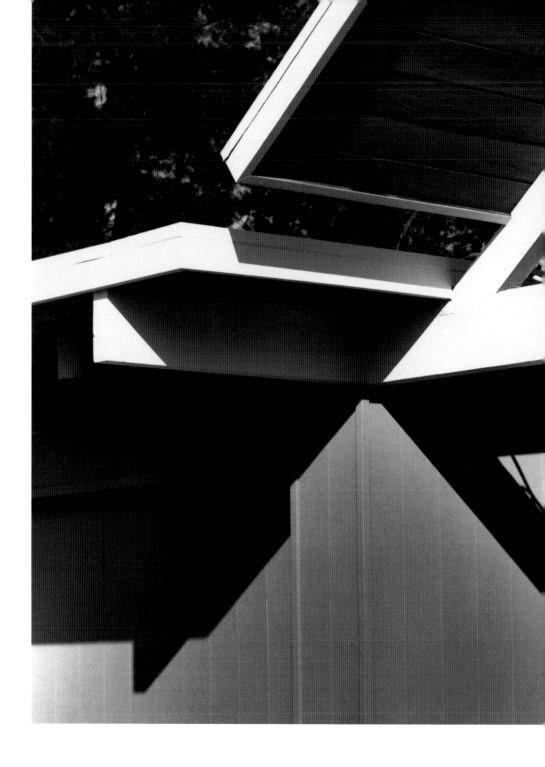

A view from the outside demonstrates the architects'
concept to have the Eichler home and living encompass
the space from lot-line to lot-line, rather than from wall
to wall. Capturing that space was a continuing hallmark
of the Eichler home.

Concrete slab foundations and open-beam ceilings make kitchen and bath remodeling a challenge, yet the timeless quality of the original design can be maintained and enhanced through tasteful redesign and the use of elegant, compatible materials.

Eichler bathrooms, not
noted for spaciousness,
can be made to feel both
spacious and elegant by
creative redesign and the
use of handsome materials.

A line drawing of the typical open-beamed ceiling contrasts with the vivid colors of 1950s decor and appointments.

defeat, Adlai Stevenson sparked the formulation of a great many liberal Democratic clubs in California. As my father's wealth grew, he became a substantial financial contributor to several candidates, notably former governor Pat Brown, Congressman Don Edwards, and Eugene McCarthy. He also gave considerable sums to liberal causes like the American Civil Liberties Union. He even helped Kennedy after the bitterness of the 1960 Democratic Convention receded. But Stevenson remained his political idol, not so much because of his stance on issues, which was quite conservative, but because of his wonderful wit.

On only one occasion did my father ever travel and not keep constant tabs on what was going on in the business. He was a delegate to the 1956 Democratic Convention in Chicago. Stevenson was sure to be the presidential nominee, but broke with tradition by throwing open to the delegates the election of his running mate. The convention went into an uproar as Kennedy, Humphrey, and Kefauver waged a close and exciting battle. I tried to contact my father by telephone for three days. Finally he called. "What the hell happened to you?" I asked. "Why didn't you call me?" He laughed and replied, "Listen, I didn't have time. I've never had so much fun with my clothes on."

Eichler Homes went bankrupt in 1967. My father used the few hundred thousand dollars he still had to start an operation building small tracts, or custom "Eichlers." For five years he made a modest profit, but increasing external difficulties, declining health (he had long suffered from heart disease), advancing age, and the 1973–75 recession ultimately overwhelmed him. He died in 1974.

Merchant builders, or any real estate developers, can be divided into two broad categories. One group is motivated entirely by greed. Its members concentrate on making money and, as they accumulate large sums, become increasingly concerned with insulating themselves against loss while still adding to their fortunes. Such people shun publicity unless they deem it useful to marketing a project or unless they have begun to position their companies for total or partial sale. One of the most successful practitioners of this ethos was Larry Weinberg, who entered homebuilding shortly after military service in World War II and who sold his company, Larwin, twenty years later for $200 million. In 1963 my wife and I went to dinner with Larry and his wife in Beverly Hills. We strolled after dining. As Larry related an entirely innocuous business incident, he leaned his head toward me and lowered his voice, even though no

Opposite page: The light coming from clerestory windows reflected on painted white paneling illuminates the entire home, including a work area, in the ubiquitous all purpose room. The floors of this home have been resurfaced with oak parquet.

A straightforward triangular expansion in the kitchen area was the genesis of this very creative and warm kitchen remodel.

Philippine mahogany wall paneling graced the walls of the Eichler home from the early 1950s to the mid 1960s. The mahogany's golden patina of age seen here, has, in many homes, been removed with restaining techniques of various colors.

A familiar facade seen
in many Eichler enclaves
after the mid 1950s.

Opposite page: The golden patina of aged mahogany paneling blends beautifully with the repainted ceiling, and ceramic tiled resurfaced flooring.

Post-and-beam construction allows for glass panels to abut wooden panels at corner junctions, as seen here. Such construction techniques are inherent in the "pavilion, bringing the outdoors in" design.

one was within a hundred yards of us and even our wives had stopped to look in a shop window. Secrecy was simply a habit. Only when Larry decided it was time to cash in, and let some sucker financial giant pay him a huge multiple on projected earnings, did he suddenly seek publicity.

The other builder group is in the business primarily for fame, not fortune. Donald Trump, whose initial dealings with Penn Central properties I handled, and Bill Levitt, whose company I ran from 1975 to 1980, after it had been sold to ITT, are classic examples of the type. They conduct their business and what most would consider their "private" lives entirely in public. They crave attention, assuming—correctly it seems—that thousands of journalists and millions of their fellow citizens are fascinated with even the most trivial details of their every act. Men like Trump and Levitt achieve substantial financial success. And they spend money lavishly on yachts—each owned the world's largest private yacht for a time—and on houses, wives, and so on. The only enjoyment they derive from such conspicuous consumption, however, is public attention. Neither business success nor the material possessions and services it facilitates have any intrinsic value to a Trump or a Levitt. Their addiction is being noticed, and they

The relatively mild California climate enables the Eichler atrium to become part of the living space—and design for living—many months of the year. This home and its atrium space provide a good example of an artful utility of this private space.

buy to retain and expand their audience. Like any addict, they raise the stakes until they fail.

I have considerable admiration for the talents and the accomplishments of developers from both groups. Bill Levitt, Larry Weinberg, and a host of other merchant builders started with nothing and greatly improved the efficiency of American residential construction and merchandising. Because of their drive, their ingenuity, and their organizational ability, they were—for the first time—able to bring better, more affordable housing to millions of people. My father was one of these men, but he did not fit into either category. Like Weinberg, he wanted wealth and security. Like Levitt and Trump, he sought and gained acclaim. Unlike the latter, he wanted money to enjoy well-designed homes, cars, clothes, fine art, and good food well served. From these he got great pleasure. It never occurred to him to invite journalists to report on these aspects of his life. He valued them for the lift they gave him. He did want and need respect for providing a unique housing product. That desire drove him to create Eichler Homes, at which he succeeded beyond his dreams; that same desire drove him to central-city apartments, at which he failed.

Both the dedicated wealth accumulators and the
maniacal publicity hounds conduct themselves
according to the dictates of American culture. On
one hand, we expect businessmen to seek maximum monetary gain, which, we know, requires
keeping one's cards close to the vest. That is how
a Weinberg plays and wins; we admire him for
doing so. On the other hand, we also demand
juicy tidbits about our heroes. The Levitts and
Trumps give them to us for whatever period they
can continue their ascent. When they fall, we turn
our attention immediately to others on the way
up. The fallen return to oblivion. My father was
much more his own man, who tried at least to
ignore the culture's constraints. It brought him
down in the end, but not before he put up a valiant
fight against it. There are far worse legacies a
father could leave a son. I cherish mine a little
more each day.

Index

The roofline reflection seen in the large expanse of glass appears almost as a phantom atrium opening in this art-filled living space. The open, pavilion-like space of many Eichler designs are well suited for displaying works of art. It very often complements the work, rather than compete or interfere with it.

Acknowledgments

This book is not only a collaborative effort between three authors, it is also a collaboration between the authors and many Eichler homeowners. We wish to extend our sincere gratitude to those homeowners who permitted our photography of their home's interior, so that the ambiance of those interiors could also be seen. They deserve special mention.

Joel & Miriam Bennett
Ethel & Julius Blank
Richard & Mary Cornwell
Lena & Herman De Kessel
Bob & Donna DeVries
Paul J. Feder
Maureen & Richard Hamner
Midge & Sylvan Heuman
Matt Kahn
William & Louise Keough
Regina Kriss
Jerry & Sheri Leonhart
Paul & Betty Lufkin
Karen Cullen & Mark Marcinik
Bob & Virginia McKim
Terry & Michael McMahon
Sue & Jerry Olson
Anna-Lise Pedersen
Russell & Moira Quacchia
Herman & Christine Ranes
Terence & Robin Roche
Linda & Tony Rostron
Tom & Barbara Shaw
Daniel & Bonnie Shurman
Angela Siddall
Marcie Singhaus
Sam & Marlene Smidt
Betty & Michael Sproule
Peter & Dagi Teschner
Ruut & Johanna van den Hoed
Jolaine & Jack Woodson